In Their Own Words

The Wisdom and Passion of Our Founding Fathers

A Book to Share
with Your Children and Grandchildren

Edward R. Nasello

In Their Own Words:
The Wisdom and Passion of Our Founding Fathers

Copyright © 2011 by Edward R. Nasello
Proof Perfect, LLC.

Author: Edward R. Nasello
Associate Editor: Emily Nasello

Photos provided courtesy of Emily Nasello.
Cover art design by Edward R. Nasello.

Rediscover America at *www.american-anthem.com*.

Library of Congress Control Number: 2010941954

ISBN 10: 0-9831898-0-3
ISBN 13: 978-0-9831898-0-0

To my daughters, Emily and Madison,
for being the inspiration to write this book;

To my loving wife, Fran,
for her encouragement and support …

To God the Almighty,
for the divine inspiration He has
given unto patriots from every
generation—past and present—
who have labored tirelessly to
establish and defend a nation
where the common man is king
and those who lead are but
servants of the people. From His
inspiration, our founding fathers
gave birth to the miracle of
America. May we each in our own
time dedicate ourselves to the
cause of preserving what so many
others have lived for and died for—
the American dream.

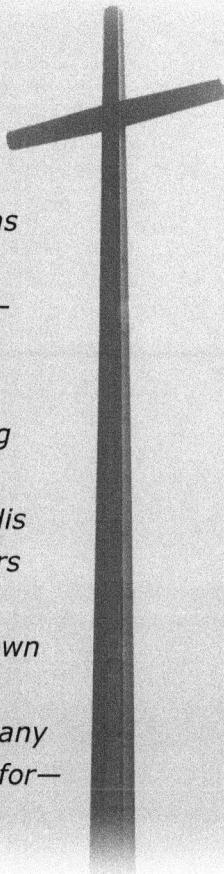

"This will be the best security for maintaining our liberties. A nation of well-informed men who have been taught to know and prize the rights which God has given them cannot be enslaved. It is in the religion of ignorance that tyranny reigns."

- Dr. Henry Stuber
(From *Works of the Late Doctor Benjamin Franklin*)

Table of Contents

Foreword

The history of the United States is rich in important lessons that must be learned and passed on from one generation to the next. Our history is more than just a list of important names and dates. It is more than a series of events with no context. To truly understand our history, a much deeper understanding of our past is required. This deeper understanding can often be found in the words of those who authored the story of our nation. Some of these words can be found in the Declaration of Independence and in our Constitution. They can also be found in the speeches and writings of those who founded our great nation.

By studying the words of our founders, we can better understand our past and the events that shaped the history of our nation. The words of our founders contain both wisdom and passion. This wisdom and passion has taken our nation on a great journey that has rewarded us with many blessings. It is reasonable to conclude that we may continue on this journey provided that we do not forget the wisdom and passion of our founders.

The men who founded our nation were great students of history. If their hopes and dreams for our nation are to endure, we too must be students of history. We must capture their wisdom and passion and make it our own.

It is the purpose of this book to inspire a hunger and thirst for greater knowledge about our past. The words of our founders, as contained in this book, are provided as a means to encourage the exploration of the values and principles upon which our nation has been founded. Questions and commentary have also been provided in hope of prompting further discussion about the ideals that were so important to our founders and have paved the road for the course of our history. Through a personal commitment to these same ideals, may we also pave the road to our destiny.

"Whoever wishes to foresee the future must consult the past; for human events ever resemble those of preceding times. This arises from the fact that they are produced by men who ever have been, and ever shall be, animated by the same passions, and thus they necessarily have the same results."

- Niccolò Machiavelli

Part I

The Declaration of Independence

America's long journey towards independence can be traced back to the early 1600s. At first, only a few hundred settlers traveled from England to the North American continent. The first to arrive settled in Jamestown, Virginia in 1607. Soon after, in 1620, the Pilgrims arrived at Plymouth, Massachusetts. In the years that followed, thousands upon thousands of settlers came to the shores of North America from England. All came in search of a new beginning. Many came seeking religious freedom and liberty.

Life for the first settlers did not come easy. They faced disease and famine, as well as wars and disputes over land. But by the early 1700s, thirteen colonies were firmly established in North America. The people who lived in these colonies farmed their land and established businesses, yet they were still subject to the rule of the King of England. Over time, tensions grew. The colonists, who believed many of their rights were being deprived by the king, were resentful of the taxes levied on them and the presence of British soldiers on American soil. Before long, anger and resentment led to conflict and violence. It was against this backdrop that the founders of our nation stepped to the forefront.

In May of 1775, delegates from the thirteen colonies arrived in Philadelphia to convene a meeting of the Second Continental Congress. By July of 1776, a formal Declaration of Independence from Great Britain was drafted and approved by the colonies.

Why was the Declaration of Independence so important in 1776?

The Declaration of Independence told the rest of the world that all thirteen colonies were united in declaring their independence. It let the King of England know that the colonies were prepared to fight, even to die, for their independence.

The brave men who signed the Declaration of Independence did so at great personal risk—a fact that Benjamin Franklin reminded the other leaders of the colonies when he said:

"We must all hang together, or assuredly we shall all hang separately."

Signing the Declaration of Independence was just one of many steps in a difficult journey that would lead to the independence of the thirteen colonies. But its important symbolic meaning helped to unite the American colonists as they prepared to fight for their freedom.

Why is the Declaration of Independence so important today?

Most of us have been taught about the importance of the document itself and the importance of July 4th as the recognized date of our birth as a nation. We even celebrate the 4th of July as a national holiday. We understand that the signing of the Declaration of Independence was important to the United States becoming an independent nation. But how many of us truly know the meaning of the words within this historical document?

Even today, the words found within the Declaration of Independence hold important meaning to Americans. These words remind us of the value of independence. The men who wrote the Declaration of Independence were not just speaking about the independence of a nation. They were also speaking about the independence of each individual person.

Though we live in a nation of great freedom and liberty, our freedoms and liberties are under attack all of the time—from other nations and even from within. The Declaration of Independence should serve as a reminder to us all that the struggle for true independence is an ongoing struggle that must be carried on by each generation.

Understanding the Declaration of Independence

The Declaration of Independence can be divided into five parts:

1. The Introduction
    This is the opening paragraph. It explains the reason for drafting the document.

2. The Preamble
    The preamble declares the rights that the colonists believed all people have.

3. The Indictment
    This part of the document lists how the rights of the colonists had been abused.

4. The Denunciation
    The denunciation explains that the colonists believed a separation between the colonies and Great Britain was necessary.

5. The Conclusion
    This is the formal declaration of the colonists to be independent from the rule of the king and the British government.

On the pages that follow are excerpts from the Declaration of Independence that highlight the desires and beliefs of our founders. For a more comprehensive understanding of the Declaration of Independence, reading the complete document in its entirety is encouraged.

Words to Remember

(excerpts from the Declaration of Independence)

The Introduction

When, in the Course of human events, it becomes necessary for one people to dissolve the political bonds which have connected them with another, and to assume among the powers of the earth, the separate and equal station to which the Laws of Nature and of Nature's God entitle them, a decent respect to the opinions of mankind requires that they should declare the causes which impel them to the separation.

The Preamble

We hold these truths to be self-evident, that all men are created equal, that they are endowed by their Creator with certain unalienable Rights, that among these are Life, Liberty and the pursuit of Happiness. —That to secure these rights, Governments are instituted among Men, deriving their just powers from the consent of the governed,—That whenever any form of Government becomes destructive to these ends, it is the Right of the People to alter or to abolish it, and to institute new Government laying its foundation on such principles and organizing its powers in such form, as to them shall seem most likely to effect their Safety and Happiness ...

The Indictment

The history of the present King of Great Britain is a history of repeated injuries and usurpations, all having in direct object the establishment of an absolute Tyranny over these States ...

He has refused his Assent to Laws, the most wholesome and necessary for the public good ...

He has combined with others to subject us to a jurisdiction foreign to our constitution, and unacknowledged by our laws; giving his Assent to their Acts of pretended Legislation:

> *For cutting off our Trade with all parts of the world;*

> *For imposing Taxes on us without our Consent;*

> *For depriving us in many cases, of the benefits of Trial by Jury; ...*

> *For taking away our Charters, abolishing our most valuable Laws, and altering fundamentally the Forms of our Governments ...*

In every stage of these Oppressions We have Petitioned for Redress in the most humble terms: Our repeated Petitions have been answered only by repeated injury. A Prince, whose character is thus marked by every act which may define a Tyrant, is unfit to be the ruler of a free people.

The Denunciation

We have warned [our British brethren] from time to time of attempts by their legislature to extend an unwarrantable jurisdiction over us …

They too have been deaf to the voice of justice and of consanguinity. We must, therefore, acquiesce in the necessity, which denounces our Separation, and hold them, as we hold the rest of mankind, Enemies in War, in Peace Friends.

The Conclusion

We, therefore, the Representatives of the united States of America, in General Congress, Assembled, appealing to the Supreme Judge of the world for the rectitude of our intentions, do, in the Name, and by Authority of the good People of these Colonies, solemnly publish and declare, That these United Colonies are, and of Right ought to be Free and Independent States …

And for the support of this Declaration, with a firm reliance on the protection of divine Providence, we mutually pledge to each other our Lives, our Fortunes and our sacred Honor.

Names to Remember

Here is a list of the brave men from each of the thirteen colonies who had the wisdom and courage to sign the Declaration of Independence. To these 56 patriots, we owe a debt of eternal gratitude.

Connecticut:
> Roger Sherman, Samuel Huntington, William Williams, Oliver Wolcott

Delaware:
> Caesar Rodney, George Read, Thomas McKean

Georgia:
> Button Gwinnett, Lyman Hall, George Walton

Maryland:
> Samuel Chase, William Paca, Thomas Stone, Charles Carroll of Carrollton

Massachusetts:
> John Hancock, Samuel Adams, John Adams, Robert Treat Paine, Elbridge Gerry

New Hampshire:
> Josiah Bartlett, William Whipple, Matthew Thornton

New Jersey:
> Richard Stockton, John Witherspoon, Francis Hopkinson, John Hart, Abraham Clark

New York:
William Floyd, Philip Livingston,
Francis Lewis, Lewis Morris

North Carolina:
William Hooper, Joseph Hewes, John Penn

Pennsylvania:
Robert Morris, Benjamin Rush,
Benjamin Franklin, John Morton,
George Clymer, James Smith, George Taylor,
James Wilson, George Ross

Rhode Island:
Stephen Hopkins, William Ellery

South Carolina:
Edward Rutledge, Thomas Heyward, Jr.,
Thomas Lynch, Jr., Arthur Middleton

Virginia:
George Wythe, Richard Henry Lee,
Thomas Jefferson, Benjamin Harrison,
Thomas Nelson, Jr., Francis Lightfoot Lee,
Carter Braxton

Learn More

To acquire a better understanding of the Declaration of Independence, make a commitment to learn more about this historic document.

Here are a few suggestions:

- Each 4th of July, take a few moments to read the Declaration of Independence with your family.

- Learn about the events that led up to the American colonists seeking independence from Great Britain. Read about the Stamp Act, the Townshend Acts, the Intolerable Acts, the Boston Massacre, and the Boston Tea Party.

- Read about Samuel Adams and Thomas Paine to learn how they rallied American colonists to the cause of independence from Great Britain.

- Learn about the role that Thomas Jefferson, John Adams, and Benjamin Franklin played in writing the Declaration of Independence.

Part II

The Constitution

The Treaty of Paris, in 1783, formally ended the American Revolution. But for our founders, in many ways, winning independence from Great Britain was the easy part in establishing a new nation. Creating a government that would unite the states and protect the freedom and liberty of the American people for generations to come was an even greater challenge.

In the years that followed the American Revolution, there was much debate and disagreement among the states over how best to establish a government for the people and by the people.

Finally, in the summer of 1787, delegates from the states met in Philadelphia to draft a document that would serve as the supreme law of the United States.

In drafting the United States Constitution, our founders were very mindful of the fact that there was a danger in giving too much power to one central federal government. Yet, they knew that a strong federal government was needed to unite the states. They believed that this would be the best hope for protecting the freedom and liberty of the American people. With this in mind, the founders took great care to craft a constitution that respected the rights of individuals and states, while limiting the role of the federal government.

What Makes Our Constitution So Special?

Many nations have crafted their own constitutions over the years. But very few have lasted as long, and none have been as successful at protecting the rights of the people as the Constitution of the United States.

Since the founding of our nation, constitutions developed by other nations have lasted an average of about seventeen years. In contrast, the Constitution of the United States has endured for well over 200 years. This is not without reason.

The United States Constitution is a well-thought-out and well-written document that is built upon sound principles. Furthermore, it is simple and easy to understand. The original document was printed on only four pages.

One of the most important purposes that the document serves is that it establishes a separation of powers between three branches of government—legislative, executive, and judicial. This separation of powers ensures that no one person (or group of people) acquires too much power. It is a principle that has served our nation well for over 200 years, and therefore we should continue to honor.

What is the Bill of Rights?

When our founders created the Constitution, they wanted to do more than just explain the role of government. They also wanted to make sure that the rights of the people would be protected. Therefore, they created the Bill of Rights and added it to the Constitution.

The Bill of Rights consists of the first ten amendments to our Constitution. The Bill of Rights is very special because it protects the freedoms and liberties of each individual.

The Bill of Rights is also special because it is based on the *natural laws* of mankind. Natural laws are the laws of nature and the world. These are the laws that come from a divine creator—God.

Because our Constitution (which includes the Bill of Rights) is based on natural law, the foundational ideas expressed in the document are timeless. Although the world may continue to change, the core principles of the Constitution still apply to our lives today, just as they did to the lives of those who crafted the document over 200 years ago.

Understanding Our Constitution

The United States Constitution can be divided into three main parts:

1. The Preamble

    The Preamble can be thought of as an introduction to the Constitution. In just one sentence, the preamble explains in a powerful way the purpose for establishing the Constitution.

2. The Articles of the Constitution

    There are seven articles in our Constitution. Articles I, II, and III provide the foundation for the concept of separation of powers. Articles IV through VII deal primarily with the interaction between federal and state governments and the process of amending the Constitution.

3. The Amendments

    Amendments are additions or changes to the original Constitution. The first ten amendments are known as the Bill of Rights.

On the pages that follow are excerpts from the United States Constitution that underscore some of the key provisions that serve as the blueprint for our way of life. For a more comprehensive understanding of the Constitution, reading the complete document in its entirety is encouraged.

Words to Remember

(excerpts from the United States Constitution)

<u>The Preamble</u>

We the People of the United States, in Order to form a more perfect Union, establish Justice, insure domestic Tranquility, provide for the common defense, promote the general Welfare, and secure the Blessings of Liberty to ourselves and our Posterity, do ordain and establish this Constitution for the United States of America.

<u>Articles of the Constitution</u>

Article I:

All legislative Powers herein granted shall be vested in a Congress of the United States, which shall consist of a Senate and House of Representatives ...

Article II:

The executive Power shall be vested in a President of the United States of America ...

The President shall be Commander in Chief of the Army and Navy of the United States, and of the Militia of the several States, when called into the actual Service of the United States ...

Article III:

The judicial Power of the United States, shall be vested in one supreme Court, and in such inferior Courts as the Congress may from time to time ordain and establish ...

The judicial Power shall extend to all Cases, in Law and Equity, arising under this Constitution, the Laws of the United States, and Treaties made, or which shall be made, under their Authority ...

Bill of Rights

Amendment I:

Congress shall make no law respecting an establishment of religion, or prohibiting the free exercise thereof; or abridging the freedom of speech, or of the press; or the right of the people peaceably to assemble, and to petition the Government for a redress of grievances.

Amendment II:

A well regulated Militia, being necessary to the security of a free State, the right of the people to keep and bear Arms, shall not be infringed.

Amendment IV:

The right of the people to be secure in their persons, houses, papers, and effects, against unreasonable searches and seizures, shall not be violated, and no Warrants shall issue, but upon probable cause ...

Amendment V:

[No person] shall be compelled in any criminal case to be a witness against himself, nor be deprived of life, liberty, or property, without due process of law; nor shall private property be taken for public use, without just compensation.

Amendment VI:

In all criminal prosecutions, the accused shall enjoy the right to a speedy and public trial, by an impartial jury ... to be confronted with the witnesses against him ... and to have the Assistance of Counsel for his defense.

Amendment VIII:

Excessive bail shall not be required, nor excessive fines imposed, nor cruel and unusual punishments inflicted.

Amendment X:

The powers not delegated to the United States by the Constitution, nor prohibited by it to the States, are reserved to the States respectively, or to the people.

Names to Remember

Here is a list of the 39 delegates that signed the United States Constitution on September 17, 1787. Their inspired vision has provided the foundation on which our nation has been built.

Delaware:
        George Read
        Gunning Bedford, Jr.
        John Dickinson
        Richard Bassett
        Jacob Broom

Maryland:
        James McHenry
        Daniel of St. Thomas Jenifer
        Daniel Carroll

Virginia:
        John Blair
        James Madison, Jr.
        George Washington*

North Carolina:
        William Blount
        Richard Dobbs Spaight
        Hugh Williamson

South Carolina:
        John Rutledge
        Charles Cotesworth Pinckney
        Charles Pinckney
        Pierce Butler

Georgia:
William Few
Abraham Baldwin

New Hampshire:
John Langdon
Nicholas Gilman

Massachusetts:
Nathaniel Gorham
Rufus King

Connecticut:
William Samuel Johnson
Roger Sherman

New York:
Alexander Hamilton

New Jersey:
William Livingston
David Brearley
William Paterson
Jonathan Dayton

Pennsylvania:
Benjamin Franklin
Thomas Mifflin
Robert Morris
George Clymer
Thomas Fitzsimons
Jared Ingersoll
James Wilson
Gouverneur Morris

*President and deputy from Virginia

Learn More

To acquire a better understanding of our Constitution, make a commitment to learn more about this historic document.

Here are a few suggestions:

- Own a copy of the United States Constitution. Read the Constitution with another member of your family. Discuss the powers granted to each branch of government under the Constitution.

- Learn about the events that led up to the Constitutional Convention of 1787. Read about Shays' rebellion, the weaknesses and failures of the Articles of Confederation, and the Annapolis Convention.

- For a more in-depth understanding of the goals and objectives of the Constitution, read the *Federalist Papers*.

- Read about George Washington, James Madison, Alexander Hamilton, and Benjamin Franklin to learn about the contributions they made to the United States Constitution.

Part III

Our Founding Fathers

Who were our Founding Fathers?

If you asked a group of historians to define the term "founding fathers," most would likely agree that the term refers to the group of American patriots who played significant roles in achieving our nation's independence from Great Britain and in the formation of a new government. However, if you asked the same group of historians to list the names of those individuals they consider to be founding fathers, it is very unlikely that any two lists would be exactly the same.

Most of the founding fathers belong to one of two groups—the signers of the Declaration of Independence or the framers of the United States Constitution. Yet, not all of our founding fathers would fall into either group. Some played other important roles by rallying the American people to the cause of liberty and defending the rights of the colonists during the American Revolution.

Though all of our founding fathers shared a similar vision for what our nation would become, they did not always agree about the particular details regarding how best to achieve their objectives. Therefore, the founding of our nation was a collaborative effort that required much discussion and debate. Even George Washington, known as the "father of our nation," could not have given birth to the American dream without the efforts of the other founding fathers.

Together, each contributed in his own way to creating the foundation upon which our nation would be built.

Even though our founding fathers were a diverse group of individuals (soldiers, writers, inventors, businessmen, lawyers, farmers, and diplomats), they shared many core values that united them in their struggle for freedom and liberty. They might not have all shared the same religious beliefs, but they did all have a common respect for religion and morality. And though they did not know with certainty how best to establish a new government, they committed themselves to learning about different political systems and forms of government throughout the ages, in order to create the best possible form of government for our nation. Our founding fathers were well-educated men with well-defined convictions about creating a nation that would be governed by the will of the people.

Today when we look back at our founding fathers through the prism of history, they are seen as uncommon men in many regards. Being separated from these men by centuries and several generations, they can sometimes even seem to be larger-than-life characters of fiction. It can be difficult for us to see them as the real men that they were. But understanding who they were will provide us with a greater appreciation for all that they accomplished. It will also challenge us to think about all that we may accomplish.

Like all people, our founding fathers were not without flaws. But unlike most, they possessed the character, intellect, and ability to transform the course of history. In this regard, they were quite uncommon.

On the pages that follow are the words of some of our more celebrated founding fathers. These words provide insight into the values and principles in which our founding fathers believed so strongly. Acquiring an understanding and appreciation of these values and principles is essential if we wish to remain on the course that was first set for our nation over two hundred years ago.

George Washington

(February 22, 1732 – December 14, 1799)

"On the whole, his character was, in its mass, perfect, in nothing bad, in few points indifferent; and it may truly be said, that never did nature and fortune combine more perfectly to make a man great."

- Thomas Jefferson

George Washington first made his mark on America's history as a soldier and general. At the age of 20, he joined the Virginia militia and fought in the French and Indian War (1754–1763). Then, in 1775 he was unanimously named the commander in chief of the American revolutionary forces.

During the American Revolutionary War (1775–1783), Washington was able to lead his troops to victory against superior British military forces. Although Washington's Continental Army suffered many defeats early on in the war, they were able to persevere and win key battles at Saratoga and Yorktown, which ultimately led to British surrender.

After the war, Washington returned to his home at Mount Vernon to retire. However, it was soon clear that the future of the United States was still very much in doubt. There was much disagreement and conflict among the states. The nation was in need of a leader who could be trusted and respected by all. Though he did not seek the Office of the President, Washington was unanimously elected and served two terms. As president, Washington was able to unite the states and provide the stability needed to allow our nation to prosper.

For his achievements as a soldier, general, and president, George Washington has earned the honor of being called the "father of our nation."

Providence

"No country upon earth ever had it more in its power to attain these blessings than United America. Wondrously strange, then, and much to be regretted indeed would it be, were we to neglect the means, and to depart from the road, which Providence has pointed us to so plainly; I cannot believe it will ever come to pass."

Thoughts & Reflections

★ ★ ★ ★

The word *Providence* refers to "guidance that comes from God."

George Washington and many of the other founding fathers believed that the United States was destined for greatness because it is a nation guided by God. In a sense, they viewed the United States as a miracle from God.

George Washington believed that the American people had an obligation to follow the path put before them by God.

⎯⎯⎯⎯⎯⎯◦⊱⊰◦⎯⎯⎯⎯⎯⎯

Do you think George Washington was right and that the United States is a nation that has been guided by the hand of God? Are there any events in our history that support this belief?

Happiness

"Your love of liberty, your respect for the laws, your habits of industry, and your practice of the moral and religious obligations, are the strongest claims to national and individual happiness—and they will, I trust, be firmly and lastingly established."

Thoughts & Reflections

★ ★ ★ ★

In the Declaration of Independence, our founding fathers spoke of the right to pursue happiness but did not guarantee happiness itself. George Washington shared his wisdom in telling us how he believed we could achieve happiness.

George Washington saw America as a special place that was home to a special group of people. He believed that the American people were a hard working and virtuous people. He understood that a willingness to work hard, respect the law, and lead a moral and religious life was the best possible foundation for happiness. Washington believed that these qualities could be found in most Americans and was optimistic about the future of our nation and the happiness of its people.

How is the *right to pursue happiness* different from a *guarantee of happiness*?

What makes you most happy? What do you think is the key to happiness?

Patriotism

"Every post is honorable in which a man can serve his country."

Thoughts & Reflections

★ ★ ★ ★

The dictionary defines a patriot as "one who loves and loyally supports his or her own country."

There was perhaps no greater patriot in our entire nation's history than George Washington. He spent much of his life in service of his country, as a soldier and as an officer in the military. Washington commanded the utmost respect from the men who served with him. During the American Revolution, Washington once declared that he would accept no payment for his service until the war was won.

After the American Revolution had ended, George Washington was called to serve his country again— this time as president. Congress voted to pay George Washington a salary of $25,000 per year, but Washington did not wish to be paid a salary for his service and opposed this decision. Despite his strong desire to return to his home at Mount Vernon, Washington served as president for eight years.

———————————⟶◦⟋⟍◦⟵———————————

In what ways have you served your country?

What more can you do to serve your country?

Religion

"I have often expressed my sentiments, that every man, conducting himself as a good citizen, and being accountable to God alone for his religious opinions, ought to be protected in worshipping the Deity according to the dictates of his own conscience."

Thoughts & Reflections

★ ★ ★ ★

Some of the first settlers to come to America came to escape from places where they were not free to practice the religion of their choice.

Our founding fathers were determined to make the United States a place that allowed great religious freedom. People would be allowed to practice any religion.

George Washington understood that it was not the role of government to establish or promote any one religion over another.

———————⟶〰○———————

How is the United States different from places in the world where there is no religious freedom?

How would your life be different if you did not have religious freedom?

God

"*It is the duty of all Nations to acknowledge the Providence of Almighty God, to obey His will, to be grateful for His benefits, and humbly to implore His protection and favor.*"

Thoughts & Reflections

★ ★ ★ ★

Most of our founding fathers had a strong belief in religion and God. George Washington believed that as a nation, the United States had a duty to do the work of God.

Looking to the word of God for guidance and direction has helped to shape many of the principles and values upon which our nation has been founded, and has provided us with many great blessings.

How do the principles and values on which our nation has been founded reflect the word of God?

Can you think of ways in which the United States has done the work of God?

In what ways have the people of the United States been blessed by God?

National Defense

"To be prepared for war, is one of the most effectual means of preserving peace."

Thoughts & Reflections

★ ★ ★ ★

As someone who fought in many battles, George Washington knew all too well the death and destruction that accompanied war. He understood the importance of preserving peace.

George Washington believed that the best way to preserve peace was to be prepared for war. He felt it was important that the rest of the world know that the United States was ready, willing, and able to defend itself. This meant having a strong and sizeable military force.

As a man who understood matters of war and peace very well, Washington knew that to appear weak as a nation was the best way to invite war. He understood that the best chance for avoiding war would be a strong national defense.

───────⟩⟨───────

How can being prepared for war help to avoid war?

Why does appearing weak as a nation invite war?

The Constitution

"*The Constitution which at any time exists, 'till changed by an explicit and authentic act of the whole People, is sacredly obligatory upon all.*"

Thoughts & Reflections

★ ★ ★ ★

George Washington and the other founding fathers risked everything to win their independence from a nation that was ruled by a king. They were determined to create a new nation that would be ruled through the consent of the people. The Constitution was constructed as the supreme law of the land with this very much in mind.

The first three words that appear in the United States Constitution are larger than any other words and read: *We the People*. These three words call to attention the fact that the power to govern the United States is derived from the people—not a ruler or king. Furthermore, the Constitution applies equally to all citizens of the United States—no one is above the law.

———————————⊃◯⊂———————————

Why is the Constitution of the United States such an important document?

What does it mean that the power to govern the United States is derived from the people?

Religion and Morality

"Of all the dispositions and habits which lead to political prosperity, Religion and morality are indispensable supports."

Thoughts & Reflections

★ ★ ★ ★

Most political leaders today are not as comfortable in expressing the importance of religion in establishing a just and moral government as George Washington was when he was president. But Washington understood that religion and morality are essential to govern and to lead a free nation.

A person who demonstrates morality knows the difference between right and wrong. George Washington believed that morality could not be maintained without religion.

How do your religious beliefs help you to know the difference between right and wrong?

Do you think it is important for presidents and other leaders to be religious? Why or why not?

Perseverance

"We should never despair. Our Situation has before been unpromising, and has changed for the better; so, I trust, it will again. If new difficulties arise, we must only put forth new exertions and proportion our efforts to the exigency of the times."

Thoughts & Reflections

★ ★ ★ ★

One reason that George Washington was a great leader was that he faced many difficult situations without backing down or giving up. He understood that to overcome difficult circumstances it was necessary to stand strong and put forth greater effort—or as he stated it: "put forth new exertions and proportion our efforts to the exigency of the times."

During his lifetime, George Washington often succeeded when others thought he would fail. But he also failed many times as well. Throughout the American Revolution, as the commander in chief of the Continental Army, Washington lost many battles. There were times when it seemed that all was lost. However, through perseverance and persistence, George Washington led the American people to victory.

When faced with the possibility of failure, what do you usually do?

What does the word *perseverance* mean? Can you think of a time when you showed great perseverance?

The Rule of Law

"If, in the opinion of the People, the distribution or modification of the Constitutional powers be in any particular wrong, let it be corrected by an amendment in the way which the Constitution designates. But let there be no change by usurpation; for though this, in one instance, may be the instrument of good, it is the customary weapon by which free governments are destroyed."

Thoughts & Reflections

★ ★ ★ ★

The very foundation of our Constitution is the core belief that the United States is a nation governed by law—not by men. No one is above the law, and no single person has the authority to change the law.

George Washington reminds us that the Constitution has clearly defined the role of government and its proper distribution of power. Furthermore, he warns us against changing the laws that govern our nation without complying with the written words of our Constitution and honoring the rule of law.

───────⊃〰⊂───────

How is a nation that is governed by law different from a nation that is governed by men?

What is the proper way to make a modification, or change, to the United States Constitution?

America and God

"No people can be bound to acknowledge and adore the Invisible Hand, which conducts the affairs of men, more than the people of the United States. Every step by which they have advanced to the character of an independent Nation seems to have been distinguished by some token of providential agency."

Thoughts & Reflections

★ ★ ★ ★

As we look back at the history of our great country, we have the advantage of knowing how everything to this point has unfolded. But for our founding fathers, there was much uncertainty about what the United States would become. Each step along the way to its destiny was a challenge.

Among such uncertainty about the future, George Washington believed that the American people would be able to rise to each of the challenges they faced, secure in the knowledge that they would be guided by the hand of God.

Do you believe, as George Washington did, that God is the "Invisible Hand" that guides our nation?

How has God helped you in your own life to face challenges and overcome obstacles?

John Adams

(October 30, 1735 – July 4, 1826)

"This illustrious patriot has not his superior, scarcely his equal for abilities and virtue on the whole of the continent of America."

- Benjamin Rush

John Adams was a well-educated man with strong beliefs. In his early years, he was highly regarded as a gifted lawyer with great passion and ambition. In the years leading up to the Revolutionary War, Adams was an outspoken supporter of colonial rights and self-government. His stubborn manner and passion for his beliefs earned him the admiration of some while making enemies of others.

From 1774–1777, Adams served as a delegate for Massachusetts in the Continental Congress. It was during this time that Adams made his most important contributions to the cause of American independence. He wrote papers and delivered passionate speeches promoting freedom and liberty. Adams also collaborated with Thomas Jefferson and Benjamin Franklin to write the Declaration of Independence and promote its adoption. To many historians, John Adams is considered the "voice of the American Revolution."

Adams made further contributions to the American cause as a diplomat in Europe and as George Washington's vice-president, before becoming the second president of the United States in 1797. Yet, it was mainly his contributions in the years leading up to the American Revolution that have secured Adams' place in history as one of our most important founding fathers.

Government

"**Government is instituted for the common good; for the protection, safety, prosperity, and happiness of the people; and not for profit, honor, or private interest of any one man, family, or class of men; therefore, the people alone have an incontestable, unalienable, and indefeasible right to institute government; and to reform, alter, or totally change the same, when their protection, safety, prosperity, and happiness require it.**"

Thoughts & Reflections

★ ★ ★ ★

John Adams was one of the most outspoken founding fathers when it came to defining the role of government. He was very clear in expressing his belief that the government of the United States exists for the benefit of the people—not for the benefit of those who govern.

When Adams declared that the people alone have an "unalienable" right to institute a government, he was reminding us that the right to govern was bestowed on us all by God and could not be taken away by any one person or class of people. Government in the United States exists by consent of the American people and should only be changed with the consent of the people.

———————⸘———————

Why is it important for leaders and government officials to remember that government exists for the "protection, safety, prosperity, and happiness of the people"?

What are the dangers in having leaders that use their power to govern for "profit" or "private interest"?

Liberty
and Religion

"Statesmen, my dear Sir, may plan and speculate for liberty, but it is religion and morality alone, which can establish the principles upon which freedom can securely stand."

Thoughts & Reflections

★ ★ ★ ★

The word *liberty* means "to be free from the control of others." It is a concept that is easy to understand and something that we all desire. But throughout history, liberty for all people has been difficult to achieve. John Adams understood this and knew that careful planning alone would not be enough for the United States to become a nation of *liberty for all*. He understood that our nation would need to be a nation of religious and moral people.

John Adams wanted the United States to be a place that allowed great religious freedom. He also hoped that we would be a nation that embraced religion in our culture. Without religion and morality, Adams believed that *liberty for all* could not be secured.

Do you agree that religion and morality are needed to secure liberty for all? Why or why not?

Do you believe that the United States, as it is today, embraces religion? Explain.

Politics

"*I must study politics and war that my sons may have liberty to study mathematics and philosophy. My sons ought to study mathematics and philosophy, geography, natural history and naval architecture, navigation, commerce and agriculture, in order to give their children a right to study painting, poetry, music, architecture, statuary, tapestry, and porcelain.*"

Thoughts & Reflections

★ ★ ★ ★

John Adams spent most of his life trying to secure liberty for the American people and trying to establish a government that would preserve this liberty. But he did not particularly enjoy politics—in fact, there was much about it that he did not like. Yet, like our other founding fathers, Adams believed that he had an obligation to future generations of Americans.

John Adams did not choose a career in politics for his own personal gain. He chose to serve his country so that his children and their children would grow up in a better world.

Are most politicians today like John Adams, or are they different? How?

What motivates you most to do the things that you choose to do?

Morality

"*Our Constitution was made only for a moral and religious people. It is wholly inadequate to the government of any other.*"

Thoughts & Reflections

★ ★ ★ ★

The United States Constitution was written to govern a nation of free people. But establishing a government that permits great freedom calls for placing a great deal of trust in those who govern, as well as great trust in those who are governed.

John Adams believed strongly in the principles that are expressed in our Constitution, but he also knew that the type of government that it sought to establish would depend greatly on the ability of the American people to conduct themselves with morality. Those who govern, must be fair and just. Those who are governed must conduct themselves with respect to right or wrong in all that they do.

Do you conduct yourself with morality in all that you do?

Do our leaders and those who govern our nation conduct themselves with morality in all that they do?

Knowledge

"*Liberty cannot be preserved without a general knowledge among the people, who have a right, from the frame of their nature, to knowledge, as their great Creator, who does nothing in vain, has given them understandings, and a desire to know.*"

Thoughts & Reflections

★ ★ ★ ★

John Adams hoped that the United States would be a place that promoted an open exchange of information and ideas. He believed that it was important for government to act in a transparent manner so that the people were always well informed. Free speech and freedom of the press would also help to guarantee that the American people would have access to a wealth of information.

Still, even with access to information, it is the obligation of each individual person to seek the knowledge that is available. Only with knowledge are the American people well armed to preserve their liberty.

Do you think that staying informed about what is going on in the world is an obligation? Why or why not?

How do you stay informed about what is going on in the world?

Property

"The moment the idea is admitted into society that property is not as sacred as the laws of God, and that there is no force of law and public justice to protect it, anarchy and tyranny commence. If 'Thou shalt not covet' and 'Thou shalt not steal' were not commandments of Heaven, they must be made inviolable precepts in every society, before it can be civilized or made free."

Thoughts & Reflections

★ ★ ★ ★

As students of history themselves, many of our founding fathers worried that established governments often believed that they had the power to take or redistribute the property of the people for the greater good of society. John Adams clearly expressed his views to the contrary.

John Adams believed that the right to one's own property is a sacred right. What each individual works for and earns, no government or person should have the right to take away.

If individuals are deprived of the fruits of their labor, as Adams understood, it will destroy their incentive for being productive and industrious. This would undermine the very fabric of our society.

⸻

Do you feel that your right to your own personal property is secure? Or do you think this right has been violated in any way?

Law

"*No man will contend, that a nation can be free, that is not governed by fixed laws. All other government than that of permanent known laws, is the government of mere will and pleasure.*"

Thoughts & Reflections

★ ★ ★ ★

In his day, John Adams was a well-respected and admired lawyer. Few men had as much respect for the rule of law as John Adams. In fact, on one occasion in particular (following the Boston Massacre in 1770) he demonstrated just how strongly he believed in his responsibility to uphold the law.

At the time—during the years leading up to the American Revolution—there was much tension between the British and the American colonists. This tension eventually led to violence. On March 5, 1770, British soldiers fired their muskets into a crowd and were accused of murdering five Boston colonists. Although John Adams often spoke out against the British, his respect for the rule of law led him to defend the soldiers during their trial. This made John Adams unpopular with some, but also gained him even greater respect from others.

How do laws protect our liberty?

What did John Adams mean that our nation should be governed by "fixed" and "permanent" laws?

Loss
of Liberty

"A Constitution of Government once changed from Freedom, can never be restored. Liberty, once lost, is lost forever."

Thoughts & Reflections

★ ★ ★ ★

Even in a free nation, liberty is always in danger of being lost. John Adams understood that if people in positions of power were to acquire too much power, they would be unlikely to give this power back. Only by establishing a new government could liberty be restored. This is why Adams and the other founding fathers knew that it was necessary for the American colonies to seek independence from Great Britain. They had reached a point where their liberty had been lost and would be lost forever, unless the colonists formed a new government.

Under the United States Constitution established by our founding fathers, the liberty of the American people was firmly secured. But this liberty must be guarded and protected with great care by each new generation of Americans.

Do you agree with John Adams that "Liberty, once lost, is lost forever"? Why or why not?

In the United States today, are any of your liberties threatened? What can you do to guard and protect your liberties?

Education
and Freedom

"Children should be educated and instructed in the principles of freedom."

Thoughts & Reflections

★ ★ ★ ★

John Adams reminds us that *freedom* is more than just a word. It is based on the principles that form the foundation of our nation and the laws that govern us as a people—*that all men are created equal, that they are endowed by their Creator with certain unalienable rights, that among these are life, liberty and the pursuit of happiness.*

Parents have the responsibility to teach their children about freedom. Our founding fathers understood the value of freedom from their own experiences, but they also knew that each generation of Americans would need to understand the value of freedom as well for it to endure.

⁕

What does freedom mean to you?

How have you learned about the value of freedom? What experiences have helped you to understand and appreciate the value of freedom?

Democracy

"*Remember, democracy never lasts long. It soon wastes, exhausts, and murders itself. There was never a democracy yet that did not commit suicide.*"

Thoughts & Reflections

★ ★ ★ ★

The word *democracy* comes from the Greek word *dēmokratía*, which means "rule by the people." In a pure democracy, the people would govern themselves by majority rule. Although people often refer to the United States as a democracy, it is actually a *republic*. In a republic, the people elect representatives to govern or "rule" on their behalf. However, power still rests with the people, since they can elect their representatives.

John Adams and the other founding fathers strongly believed that a republic was the best form of government for a free people—not a democracy. Adams and the other founders knew from their study of history, that in a democracy, people often made unwise decisions based on the emotions of the moment. This often led to "mob rule" with people fighting among themselves for more power and control. In a republic, our founders believed, elected representatives would exercise better judgment and greater care when making decisions.

How are a democracy and a republic different?

Does democracy exist in the United States? Explain.

Slavery

"*Consenting to slavery is a sacrilegious breach of trust, as offensive in the sight of God as it is derogatory from our own honor or interest of happiness.*"

Thoughts & Reflections

★ ★ ★ ★

In the Declaration of Independence, our founding fathers stated that "all men are created equal." Yet, when it came time to draft the Constitution, no provisions were made outlawing slavery. At the time, many Americans still owned slaves—even some of our founding fathers.

John Adams and many of the other founding fathers realized that permitting slavery to continue was not consistent with the belief that all men are created equal. But, on this one important issue, they failed to act decisively. They feared that it was not possible to end slavery and still keep the states united. So they decided to leave this issue to be resolved another time. Unfortunately, this time did not arrive until after the Civil War when the 13th Amendment to the Constitution was adopted (abolishing slavery in the United States).

How do you think our history might have been different if our founding fathers took greater efforts to end slavery?

Thomas Jefferson

(April 13, 1743 – July 4, 1826)

"*The principles of Jefferson are the definitions and axioms of a free society ... [He had the] capacity to introduce into a merely revolutionary document, an abstract truth, applicable to all men and all times.*"

- Abraham Lincoln

Thomas Jefferson had a long and distinguished career in politics that included serving as the first secretary of state (1789–1793), the second vice-president (1797–1801), and the third president (1801–1809) of the United States.

Though Jefferson had many talents, he was a particularly gifted writer. He often used this talent to write about his political philosophy—in particular, his belief in the natural rights of the individual. In a political pamphlet titled *A Summary View of the Rights of British America*, Jefferson wrote at great length about the natural rights of the American colonists. He stated, "The God who gave us life, gave us liberty at the same time: the hand of force may destroy, but cannot disjoin them."

As the principal author of the Declaration of Independence, Jefferson used his beliefs about natural rights to lay the foundation of our nation. Some of his other achievements include founding the Democratic-Republican Party (which was committed to protecting states' rights and a strict interpretation of the Constitution) and negotiating the Louisiana Purchase (which more than doubled the size of the United States).

Most historians agree that Thomas Jefferson was one of the most influential founding fathers and one of our nation's greatest presidents.

Government

"*Every government degenerates when trusted to the rulers of the people alone. The people themselves, therefore, are its only safe depositories.*"

Thoughts & Reflections

★ ★ ★ ★

Thomas Jefferson played a very important role in helping to shape the government of the United States. He believed that the role of government needed to be very limited in order for the people to truly be free.

Jefferson spoke often about empowering people to govern and control their own lives. He saw government with too much power as a threat to the liberties of the American people. Like our other founding fathers, Jefferson feared that when given too much power, leaders could not be trusted to always act in the best interest of the people.

Can you think of any examples of when government has not acted in the best interest of the people?

What powers do you think should be entrusted to a government? What powers do you think should be entrusted to the people?

Commerce

"I think all the world would gain by setting commerce at perfect liberty."

Thoughts & Reflections

★ ★ ★ ★

For over 200 years, innovation has thrived in the United States. For generations, Americans have used their individual and collective talents to establish successful businesses, generate wealth, and bring new technologies to the world. None of this would have been possible if our founding fathers had not believed so strongly in the principles of *free enterprise*.

By instituting the principles of free enterprise, our founding fathers sought to allow the American people to conduct business, or commerce, without government interference. Thomas Jefferson and the other founders knew that businesses needed to succeed in order for the United States to succeed. They believed that the best way to accomplish this was to let businesses operate as freely as possible.

What does the term *free enterprise* mean?

What are the benefits of allowing businesses to operate freely? Are there times when government should limit or control business activity? If so, when?

Government and Liberty

"*The natural progress of things is for liberty to yield and government to gain ground.*"

Thoughts & Reflections

★ ★ ★ ★

Our Constitution is a well-conceived document that outlines the principles upon which liberty and freedom can endure. But Thomas Jefferson knew there was still a danger of liberty being lost. He and the other founding fathers knew from their own experiences under British rule, that over time, a government would tend to acquire more and more power from the people.

If the people of a free nation are suddenly deprived of their liberties, it is apparent and obvious and will tend to evoke an immediate response from the people. Therefore, the real danger lies in liberty that is lost gradually over time, unnoticed by most until little or no true freedom remains. Jefferson warns us to guard against yielding our liberties to government.

Do you believe that the American people have lost any of their liberties over time?

What can you do to guard against the loss of your personal liberties?

Political Parties

"*The greatest good we can do our country is to heal its party divisions and make them one people.*"

Thoughts & Reflections

★ ★ ★ ★

In a free society, people have different beliefs and objectives they wish to pursue. Political parties exist to unite people who share similar views. However, these same political parties can also divide the people of a nation.

In the United States, political parties have been around since the time of our founding fathers. Although most of the founders shared the same core beliefs, they often disagreed over specific ideas about how best to govern our nation. In fact, Thomas Jefferson and John Adams, who worked closely together to draft the Declaration of Independence, were fierce political adversaries for most of their lives.

The two major political parties that existed when our nation was founded were the *Federalists* and the *Democratic-Republicans*. Today, the two major parties are the *Democrats* and the *Republicans*.

Do you think political parties are good for our nation? Why or Why not?

Good Government

"A wise and frugal government which shall restrain men from injuring one another, shall leave them otherwise free to regulate their own pursuits of industry and improvement, and shall not take from the mouth of labor the bread it has earned. This is the sum of good government."

Thoughts & Reflections

★ ★ ★ ★

Though Thomas Jefferson often warned about the hazards of government, he also realized that government is necessary.

As Jefferson saw it, government plays an important but limited role in a free society. Our government exists to protect the rights of the people, secure our nation against all enemies, and provide law and order among the people. But our government should not impose unjust restrictions on the people or take away from the people what they have earned.

What are some things that government does that has made your life better?

Are there some things that government does that you think it should not do? Explain.

Taxes

"*To take from one, because it is thought his own industry and that of his fathers has acquired too much, in order to spare to others ... whose fathers have not exercised equal industry and skill, is to violate arbitrarily the first principle of association—the guarantee to everyone the free exercise of his industry and the fruits acquired by it.*"

Thoughts & Reflections

★ ★ ★ ★

Under the Constitution, our founding fathers granted Congress the power to collect certain taxes from the people for a few specific purposes. Article I, section 8 of the Constitution states "Congress shall have the power to lay and collect taxes ... to pay the debts and provide for the common defense and general welfare of the United States." However, as Thomas Jefferson realized, the power to tax—if not well defined and limited—could be easily abused to "take from one" in order to "spare to others."

Thomas Jefferson knew that in a free society, some people would exercise their industry and skill to acquire more wealth than others. He warned against government using taxes as a way to redistribute this wealth. Prior to the adoption of the 16th Amendment, Congress did not have the power to tax income. But now that it does, the danger in using the power of taxation to redistribute wealth is greater than ever.

What is the proper use of money collected through taxation? What is the improper use of this money?

Do you agree with Jefferson that it is wrong to "take from one" in order to "spare to others"?

Government Spending

"The same prudence which in private life would forbid our paying our own money for unexplained projects, forbids it in the dispensation of the public moneys."

Thoughts & Reflections

★ ★ ★ ★

When a person earns money through hard work and effort, he or she will tend to give careful thought about how best to spend, save, or invest this money. In general, money that is earned is valued more than money that is acquired by some other means.

Government is not a business. It does not exist to generate money through the sale of products or services. A government acquires most of its money by levying and collecting taxes. Therefore, when it spends money, it spends other people's money.

Thomas Jefferson knew that spending other people's money would be likely to invite reckless decisions about how best to spend the money. He urged that government should make decisions about spending money with the same prudence as individuals who spend their own money.

Can you think of some wise decisions government has made about spending taxpayer money? Can you think of some decisions that were not so wise?

Education

"*If a nation expects to be ignorant and free, in a state of civilization, it expects what never was and never will be.*"

Thoughts & Reflections

★ ★ ★ ★

A person who is armed with knowledge is well prepared to defend his or her own rights and liberties. A person who remains uneducated and uninformed risks being taken advantage of by those who are better educated or in positions of power.

Thomas Jefferson reminds us of the importance of education and knowledge. Jefferson points out that it is not just important to each individual, but it is important to the prosperity of our entire nation. To remain a nation of free people capable of protecting our liberties, we must make a commitment to being well educated and well informed.

How does being well educated and well informed help us to protect our liberties?

Who is responsible for making sure that you are well educated and well informed?

How can you help educate and inform others?

Debt

"We must not let our rulers load us with perpetual debt. We must make our election between economy and liberty, or profusion and servitude."

Thoughts & Reflections

★ ★ ★ ★

Debt is how much money we owe to others. *Perpetual debt* is debt that is never ending and is passed on from one generation to the next.

When government continually spends more money than it has, debt becomes perpetual. This creates a financial burden for all citizens, since most of the money that government spends comes from taxes that are collected from the people. Furthermore, money that is borrowed and spent by one generation of Americans results in debt that is passed on to the next generation of Americans to pay back.

A responsible government is one that makes sure that it is able to pay back the money that it borrows without passing this burden on to the next generation. Thomas Jefferson warns us not to allow government to burden our nation with perpetual debt.

———————————⟩∞⟨———————————

Is the United States currently burdened with *perpetual debt*? How does a nation acquire debt? How can a nation avoid perpetual debt?

What did Jefferson mean that we must choose "economy and liberty" or "profusion and servitude"?

Morality and Virtue

"Give up money, give up fame, give up science, give the earth itself and all it contains rather than do an immoral act. And never suppose that in any possible situation, or under any circumstances, it is best for you to do a dishonorable thing, however slightly so it may appear to you ... From the practice of the purest virtue, you may be assured you will derive the most sublime comforts in every moment of life, and in the moment of death."

Thoughts & Reflections

★ ★ ★ ★

Thomas Jefferson and the other founding fathers understood the importance of morality and virtue. Jefferson believed that morality and virtue needs to be as much a part of the American experience as freedom and liberty.

As individuals, leading moral and virtuous lives is personally rewarding and fulfilling. We should never compromise when it comes to choosing right over wrong. Without morality and virtue, true freedom and liberty is not possible.

Our founding fathers had a vision that our country would lead the way for others to follow. With a sense of morality, a respect for virtue, and the character of the American people, our founders believed that our nation would serve as a model for all mankind.

What does it mean to lead a moral and virtuous life? Is this the type of life that you live?

What changes can you make in your own life to become a more moral and virtuous person?

Benjamin Franklin
(January 17, 1706 – April 17, 1790)

"*He seized the lightning from Heaven and the scepter from the Tyrants.*"

- A.R.J. Turgot

Before becoming an American hero, Benjamin Franklin had already achieved success and fame as a well-respected scientist and civic leader.

As a scientist, Franklin's greatest contributions were his discoveries and theories about electricity. As a civic leader, Franklin helped to establish the first public library and the first hospital in America.

Following the early achievements in his life, Franklin became very politically active. At first, he worked to preserve the union between the colonists and the British. But as tensions grew, he became a strong supporter of American independence. In 1776, Franklin helped to draft the Declaration of Independence. A few years later, he represented the United States at the Treaty of Paris, formally ending the American Revolution in victory.

But Franklin still had more to contribute. In 1787, at the age of 81, Franklin was a delegate at the Constitutional Convention. This same year, Franklin was also elected as president of the Pennsylvania Abolition Society. One of his last public acts was to write an anti-slavery treatise in 1789.

For all of his accomplishments and influence, many students of history have come to remember Franklin as "the only president of the United States who was never president of the United States."

God

"I have lived, sir, a long time; and the longer I live, the more convincing proofs I see of this truth—that God governs in the affairs of men. And if a sparrow cannot fall to the ground without his notice, is it probable that an empire can rise without his aid?"

Thoughts & Reflections

★ ★ ★ ★

By most accounts, Benjamin Franklin was not known as a devoutly religious man. But like most of our founding fathers, Franklin did believe in God. Furthermore, he believed that God watched over and guided the people of our nation.

During the Constitutional Convention of 1787, as delegates struggled to make progress in drafting the Constitution, Benjamin Franklin asked that *"henceforth prayers imploring the assistance of Heaven, and its blessings on our deliberations, be held in this Assembly every morning."*

Though the delegates at the Constitutional Convention did not all share the same religious beliefs, most looked to a divine source for guidance.

What did Benjamin Franklin mean when he said "God governs in the affairs of men"?

Are there times when you look to God for guidance? If so, when?

Liberty

"Those who would give up essential liberty, to purchase a little temporary safety, deserve neither liberty nor safety."

Thoughts & Reflections

★ ★ ★ ★

When Benjamin Franklin and others signed the Declaration of Independence, they did so at great personal risk. Nevertheless, they were willing to do so because they valued liberty so much.

Those who lived through the troubled times of the American Revolution had a great appreciation for the freedom and liberty their generation had to fight for and die for. But in the years leading up to the Revolutionary War, some colonists were unsure what path the American people should take. They had to decide whether to fight for liberty or sacrifice liberty to live in relative security under British rule.

Benjamin Franklin warned against giving in to the temptation of giving up liberty for security. Those willing to exchange "essential liberty" for "temporary safety," as Franklin stated so directly, deserve neither liberty nor safety.

⎯⎯⎯⎯⎯⎯⎯⎯⎯⎯⎯

Do you agree with Franklin that those willing to give up "essential liberty" for "temporary safety" deserve neither? Why or why not?

Poverty

"I am for doing good to the poor, but I differ in opinion about the means. I think the best way of doing good to the poor, is not making them easy in poverty, but leading or driving them out of it. In my youth I travelled much, and I observed in different countries, that the more public provisions were made for the poor, the less they provided for themselves, and of course became poorer. And, on the contrary, the less was done for them, the more they did for themselves, and became richer."

Thoughts & Reflections

★ ★ ★ ★

Benjamin Franklin performed many charitable acts in his life and encouraged others to be charitable as well. However, he shared the belief with our other founders, that the United States should be a country that empowers individuals to acquire wealth through their own efforts. Our founding fathers did not want the United States to become a place where individuals would be dependent on government for their success and wealth.

When "public provisions" are made for the poor, Benjamin Franklin observed, those living in poverty do very little to lift themselves out of poverty. Franklin believed that the best way to lift people out of poverty was by not allowing them to become comfortable in their poverty.

How can a person become comfortable or "easy in poverty"? Why is this not a good thing?

How can you help people who live in poverty without making them comfortable in their poverty?

Virtue

"Only a virtuous people are capable of freedom. As nations become corrupt and vicious, they have more need of masters."

Thoughts & Reflections

★ ★ ★ ★

People who are honest and virtuous are people who govern themselves and their own actions. The more virtuous people are, the less need there is for them to be governed by others.

In a free society, government power is limited and is derived from the people. However, where honesty and virtue are absent, the need to be governed by others is required at the expense of individual liberties.

Benjamin Franklin understood that the United States could only preserve its freedom and liberty by being a nation of virtuous people.

———————⟶⟨✐⟩⟵———————

Do you agree with Franklin that freedom can only exist when people are virtuous? Why or why not?

Can you think of any freedoms that you have lost because others have not always acted in an honest or virtuous way? Explain.

Religion

"*Here is my creed: I believe in one God, the creator of the universe. That he governs it by his Providence. That he ought to be worshipped. That the most acceptable service we render to him is doing good to his other children. That the soul of man is immortal, and will be treated with justice in another life respecting its conduct in this. These I take to be the fundamental points in all sound religion.*"

Thoughts & Reflections

★ ★ ★ ★

Benjamin Franklin, although not generally regarded as a devoutly religious man, openly shared his religious beliefs with others. He understood that religion is important and provides clarity and purpose for those who believe in God.

Benjamin Franklin believed that God guides us in our lives and that we are obligated to do good unto others. By leading good lives and worshipping God, Franklin believed that the immortal soul of each person would be "treated with justice in another live."

Do you feel comfortable sharing your religious beliefs with others, just as Benjamin Franklin often did? Why or why not?

Is religion important in your life?

What did Franklin mean when he said "the soul of man is immortal, and will be treated with justice in another life respecting its conduct in this"?

Leading the Way

"*It is a common observation here that our cause is the cause of all mankind, and that we are fighting for their liberty in defending our own.*"

Thoughts & Reflections

★ ★ ★ ★

During the American Revolution, the American people fought to defend liberty. This was not just the cause of all Americans, but the cause of all mankind.

While in France seeking to strengthen relations with the French people, Benjamin Franklin observed that there was a hunger for liberty among the people throughout the world. Franklin and the other founding fathers knew that the world was watching and the events that were taking place in America would shape the future of the world in a significant way.

The victory of the American people over the British, at the conclusion of the Revolutionary War, was a victory for all mankind. It marked the beginning of a new era, where liberty would prosper in places it had never existed before. As it still does to this day, in 1776 the United States led the way to liberty.

———————⊃◯⊂———————

Throughout history, what actions has the United States taken to defend liberty?

Why do the actions of the United States have such an important impact on all of mankind?

National Defense

"*The Way to secure Peace is to be prepared for War. They that are on their guard, and appear ready to receive their adversaries, are in much less danger of being attacked than the supine, secure, and negligent.*"

Thoughts & Reflections

★ ★ ★ ★

In the years leading up to the American Revolution and the years that followed, the founding generation of Americans faced many potential threats to their liberty and security. The threat of war was constant. Benjamin Franklin knew that it was important for our nation to take the necessary steps to establish a powerful military capable of defending itself against all threats.

Franklin believed that one of the best ways of securing peace was to be prepared for war. But it is important to understand that *to prepare for war* does not mean the same as *to seek war*. Rather, it is an acknowledgment that one of the best ways for a nation to secure peace is to let its adversaries know that it is willing and able to do whatever is necessary to defend itself.

⸻

What threats to the security of the United States exist today? How can we defend ourselves against these threats?

When is it necessary for a nation to go to war?

James Madison

(March 16, 1751 – June 28, 1836)

"[James Madison was] one of the pillars and ornaments of his country and of his age ... [he nobly fulfilled] his destinies as a man and a Christian. He has improved his own condition by improving that of his country and his kind."

- John Quincy Adams

In the years leading up to and following the American Revolution, James Madison was a well-respected politician and political philosopher. He served as a member of Virginia's House of Delegates and was elected to the first United States House of Representatives. Madison also served as Thomas Jefferson's Secretary of State (1801–1809) and was elected as the fourth president of the United States (1809–1817).

Although James Madison did have the distinction of becoming president of the United States, his most significant contributions were made some years earlier as a delegate from Virginia. At the Constitutional Convention of 1787, as one of the authors of our Constitution, Madison played an important role in helping to shape a strong national government that distributed power among three branches and governed through the consent of the people.

Following the Constitutional Convention, Madison co-authored the *Federalist Papers* (with Alexander Hamilton and John Jay) to promote ratification of the Constitution. He also introduced the Bill of Rights to Congress, to secure individual rights.

For the role he played in drafting and promoting the Constitution, James Madison is recognized by many scholars as the "father of the Constitution."

States' Rights

"*The powers delegated by the proposed Constitution to the federal government are few and defined. Those which are to remain in the State governments are numerous and indefinite.*"

Thoughts & Reflections

★ ★ ★ ★

When our founding fathers gathered to write our Constitution, they were very uneasy about giving power to a federal government for fear that such a government would trample over the rights of the people. But our founders did realize that a federal government was necessary to unite the states and defend our nation in times of conflict or war.

The solution that our founding fathers reached was to establish a federal government with few powers that are clearly defined within the Constitution. However, as James Madison pointed out, the powers that ought to remain with the states are numerous and indefinite. Consequently, the 10th Amendment states that any powers not granted to the federal government under the Constitution are reserved to the states or the people.

What is the difference between state government and federal government?

Why do you think Madison and the other founding fathers wanted state governments to be given more powers than the federal government?

God

"*The belief in a God All Powerful wise and good, is so essential to the moral order of the World and to the happiness of man, that arguments which enforce it cannot be drawn from too many sources.*"

Thoughts & Reflections

★ ★ ★ ★

James Madison believed strongly in a powerful and wise God. He points to the fact that many arguments can be made to support a belief in God and that such a belief is essential to the happiness of man.

Many of the other founding fathers shared the same belief as Madison. They did not just simply speak of their belief in God, but also expressed their opinion that a belief in God was essential to a moral society. Their vision for a free and prosperous nation depended greatly on the United States being a moral nation that believed in the *laws of nature's God* (often referred to by our founding fathers as "natural law"). Both the Declaration of Independence and the Constitution of the United States were written with respect to what many of our founding fathers believed were the laws of nature's God.

Do you agree with Madison that a belief in a God that is wise and good is essential to the moral order of the world? Why or why not?

What laws do you believe to be *laws of nature's God*? What laws passed on to us by our founding fathers appear to be based on these laws?

Government

"*If men were angels, no government would be necessary. If angels were to govern men, neither external nor internal controls on government would be necessary. In framing a government which is to be administered by men over men, the great difficulty lies in this: you must first enable the government to control the governed; and in the next place oblige it to control itself.*"

Thoughts & Reflections

★ ★ ★ ★

James Madison points out both the need for government and the challenge in establishing a government.

The need for government exists, as Madison implied, because people are not "angels." Laws are needed to protect the rights of the people and to protect people from one another. Government is therefore needed to establish and enforce these laws.

The great challenge lies in establishing a government that is able to exercise control of itself when entrusted with the power to govern the lives of others.

———————————⌒⌒———————————

Why is government necessary in a free country?

What concern did Madison have about a government "administered by men over men"?

Commerce

"*I own myself the friend to a very free system of commerce, and hold it as a truth, that commercial shackles are generally unjust, oppressive and impolitic—it is also a truth, that if industry and labour are left to take their own course, they will generally be directed to those objects which are the most productive, and this in a more certain and direct manner than the wisdom of the most enlightened legislature could point out.*"

Thoughts & Reflections

★ ★ ★ ★

To engage in commerce is to own or operate a business. It was important to our founding fathers that the United States would become a nation that allowed its people to engage freely in business and commerce. They understood that this was important to the prosperity of the nation and its people.

James Madison shared a belief with the other founders that businesses that are free to "take their own course" are likely to be most productive. Furthermore, Madison believed that it was unjust, oppressive, and impolitic (unwise) for commerce to be "shackled" by government.

———————⟶◦⟋⟍◦———————

Do you agree with Madison that businesses "left to take their own course" will be more productive than if they are directed by "the wisdom of the most enlightened legislature"? Why or why not?

Federalism and State Sovereignty

"Each State, in ratifying the Constitution, is considered as a sovereign body, independent of all others, and only to be bound by its own voluntary act. In this relation, then, the new Constitution will, if established, be a FEDERAL, and not a NATIONAL constitution."

Thoughts & Reflections

★ ★ ★ ★

In 1787 and 1788, James Madison, Alexander Hamilton, and John Jay wrote a series of essays referred to as the *Federalist Papers*. The purpose of these essays was to persuade the people of New York to ratify the Constitution. In the Federalist Paper Number 39, Madison addresses the difference between a *federal* and *national* constitution.

Under a federal constitution, Madison points out that each state remains a "sovereign body" that is independent of each other, but that all states voluntarily unite under one central government— a federal government. This is in contrast to a national constitution, which would govern all the people of the United States as one collective whole.

It was extremely important to Madison and the other founders that state sovereignty be protected under the Constitution.

───────── ⟫⟋⟋⟋⟨ ─────────

What is state sovereignty? Why is it important?

What is federalism? Does it protect state sovereignty?

Providence and
Divine Inspiration

"It is impossible for the man of pious reflection not to perceive in it [the Constitution] a finger of that Almighty hand which has been so frequently and signally extended to our relief in the critical stages of the revolution."

Thoughts & Reflections

★ ★ ★ ★

From the first colonists who arrived in North America in search of a better life, to the brave patriots who fought for our independence in the American Revolution, the path that led to the founding of our nation was a long and difficult struggle. As James Madison saw it, the American people were guided through these difficult times by *Providence*, or the hand of God.

During the summer of 1787, several of our founding fathers gathered to draft a Constitution that would unite our nation and protect the rights of the people. The task was not easy and at times it seemed that the efforts of our founders might fail. In reflecting on the difficult task of drafting the Constitution, Madison once again acknowledged the presence of the hand of God. Madison and many of the other founding fathers saw the United States Constitution as a work of *divine inspiration*.

Do you believe that the founding of our nation was an act of *Providence*? Why or why not?

What is *divine inspiration*? Do you believe that our Constitution is a work of divine inspiration?

Religion

"*The civil rights of none shall be abridged on account of religious belief or worship, nor shall any national religion be established, nor shall the full and equal rights of conscience be in any manner, or on any pretext, infringed.*"

Thoughts & Reflections

★ ★ ★ ★

For James Madison and the other founding fathers, protecting the individual's right to freedom of religion was of great significance. It is not by coincidence that the 1st Amendment of the Bill of Rights begins with the words "Congress shall make no law respecting an establishment of religion, or prohibiting the free exercise thereof."

The words and actions of our founding fathers make it clear it was their intent that religion would be an important part of the American experience. They understood that the values and virtues that form the foundation of religion are also essential to the foundation of a free nation. Yet, our founders knew that people in positions of power might be tempted to interfere with the free exercise of religion (as they had done so many times in the past). With this in mind, the 1st Amendment was added to our Constitution, thereby securing our religious freedom.

What views did our founding fathers have about religion and religious freedom?

What does *freedom of religion* mean to you? Are you always able to express your religious beliefs freely?

Charity

"*The government of the United States is a definite government, confined to specified objects. It is not like the state governments, whose powers are more general. Charity is no part of the legislative duty of the government.*"

Thoughts & Reflections

★ ★ ★ ★

James Madison reminds us again that the role of the United States government is limited and defined. And although the powers of state governments were intended by our founding fathers to be more general and far reaching, these powers too are limited.

Though individuals should be encouraged to be charitable, Madison shared the belief with the other founders that charity is not the role of government. Charity is a *choice* and should not be *mandated*; or else it is no longer an act of charity but an infringement upon our rights.

———————⊃〜◯⊂———————

What does the word *charity* mean? What acts of charity have you recently performed for others?

When you go through difficult times, who do you look to for help? Do you rely most on government, other individuals, or yourself?

Knowledge

"**Knowledge will forever govern ignorance: And a people who mean to be their own Governors, must arm themselves with the power which knowledge gives.**"

Thoughts & Reflections

★ ★ ★ ★

Our founding fathers intended for the people of the United States to be empowered to govern their own lives through a representative government. But as Madison points out, only people who are armed with "the power which knowledge gives" are truly able to govern themselves. Those who possess knowledge will always be in a position to govern those who live in ignorance.

In the free society in which we live, we are all empowered to acquire knowledge, but we must first choose to do so and commit ourselves to the cause.

───────────⟶⟋⟍⟍───────────

Why is knowledge important if we are to govern our own lives?

Are there steps that you can take to arm yourself with greater knowledge?

Do you agree with Madison that "knowledge will forever govern ignorance"? What does this mean?

Government Spending

"I cannot undertake to lay my finger on that article of the Constitution which granted a right to Congress of expending, on the objects of benevolence, the money of their constituents."

Thoughts & Reflections

★ ★ ★ ★

The United States Constitution does grant Congress the power to collect money from the people to "pay the Debts and provide for the common Defense and general Welfare of the United States." But as James Madison points out, the Constitution does not grant Congress the power to spend the people's money "on the objects of benevolence." In other words, the Constitution does not grant Congress the power to give money it has collected as gifts or acts of charity.

It was the intent of Madison and the other founders that money collected from the people of the United States only be used for specific purposes clearly defined in the Constitution. However, over the years, Congress has spent large sums of money on what Madison would call "objects of benevolence."

Where does the money that Congress spends come from? For what purposes should this money be used?

Can you think of examples when money has been spent by Congress on "objects of benevolence"? Do you agree with Madison that this is not an appropriate use of the people's money? Why or why not?

Law

"It will be of little avail to the people, that the laws are made by men of their own choice, if the laws be so voluminous that they cannot be read, or so incoherent that they cannot be understood."

Thoughts & Reflections

★ ★ ★ ★

The United States Constitution was written so that it could be easily read and easily understood—not for the benefit of lawmakers, but for the benefit of the American people. Our founding fathers knew that if the Constitution could be easily understood, it would have a better chance of securing the full faith and confidence of the American people as the supreme law of the land.

The original handwritten text of the Constitution of the United States is only four pages in length. Today, it is not uncommon for laws written by Congress to be hundreds of pages in length. James Madison believed that when laws become this voluminous, it is a disservice to the American people. If indeed laws are written for the benefit of the people, they should be written so as to be understood by the people.

———————⊃∽⊂———————

What did Madison mean when he described some laws as "voluminous" or "incoherent"? What is the danger of laws being written in this manner?

Abridgement of Freedom

"I believe there are more instances of the abridgement of the freedom of the people, by gradual and silent encroachments of those in power, than by violent and sudden usurpations ... This danger ought to be wisely guarded against."

Thoughts & Reflections

★ ★ ★ ★

When James Madison spoke of "the abridgement of freedom" he was referring to the possibility of our individual rights being limited or lost. There are two ways in which he suggested this could happen—slowly (by gradual encroachments) or quickly (by sudden usurpations). Madison believed that the greater danger to our freedom is that it could be lost as a result of gradual and silent encroachments by those in power.

Soon after our Constitution was written, Madison and some of the other founding fathers still had concerns about the power which was being entrusted to those who would govern the people. To guard against the abridgment of our freedom, the Bill of Rights was written and adopted to amend our Constitution.

What does the term "abridgment of freedom" mean?

How does the Bill of Rights guard against the abridgment of our freedom? What are some of the rights that it protects?

Alexander Hamilton

(January 11, 1755 or 1757 – July 12, 1804)

Hamilton's birth date is disputed; generally listed as 1/11/1755 or 1/11/1757.

"Hamilton was the greatest constructive mind in all our history and I should come pretty near saying ... in the history of modern statesmen in any country."

- Henry Cabot Lodge

Like so many other founding fathers, Alexander Hamilton contributed to the American cause in many ways—including as a soldier and as a politician.

Hamilton's military career began when he joined a volunteer militia in 1775. A few years later, he became a lieutenant colonel in the Continental Army. During much of the American Revolution, he served as George Washington's personal aide.

Following the war, Hamilton became very politically active. As the states struggled to unite, he argued that a centralized government was needed to provide strength and stability. Many of Hamilton's views about government helped to shape our Constitution. As one of the principal authors of the *Federalist Papers*, Hamilton wrote at least 51 essays that helped explain the need for a strong central government. His efforts helped secure the support needed to ratify and adopt the Constitution.

During our nation's early years, Hamilton served as George Washington's secretary of the treasury, and was one of his most trusted advisors (1789–1795). He helped to establish our national banking system and encouraged commercial development. But despite all of his achievements, Alexander Hamilton is perhaps best remembered for his tragic death. During a historic duel with Aaron Burr on July 11, 1804, Hamilton was shot and fatally wounded.

The Constitution

"*If it be asked, What is the most sacred duty and the greatest source of our security in a Republic? The answer would be, An inviolable respect for the Constitution and Laws—the first growing out of the last ... A sacred respect for the constitutional law is the vital principle, the sustaining energy of a free government.*"

Thoughts & Reflections

★ ★ ★ ★

When Alexander Hamilton spoke about the Constitution, he stated that we must have a "sacred respect for the constitutional law." The words *sacred respect* underscore just how important Hamilton believed our Constitution is to our nation; for if something is sacred, it should be regarded with respect and great reverence.

Hamilton believed that all Americans have a sacred duty to uphold and defend the Constitution. We must all have a respect for the rule of law, if the Constitution is to endure. In this regard, our founding fathers viewed the Constitution as a *timeless document*. It is based in large part on principles and values that do not change over time.

—————————⊃◠⊂—————————

Do you believe that most people today have a *sacred respect* for the Constitution? What makes you think this?

Do you have a *sacred respect* for the Constitution?

In what way is the United States Constitution a *timeless document*? What does this mean?

Liberty and Inequality

"Inequality would exist as long as liberty existed ... it would unavoidably result from that very liberty itself."

Thoughts & Reflections

★ ★ ★ ★

The Constitution (particularly the Bill of Rights) was intended by our founding fathers to ensure equal opportunity but not necessarily equal results. Our founders were careful to write a Constitution that guaranteed only the *equal rights* of the people. This is very different from a *guarantee of equality*, which Alexander Hamilton points out is not possible as long as individual liberty is to be protected.

In a society that protects individual liberties, each person is free to make use of his or her talents and resources in different ways. Thus, different results will be achieved by each individual. Hamilton realized that it is unrealistic to expect perfect equality in all aspects of our lives if people are free to make decisions that will impact their own successes and failures.

———————⟨✑⟩———————

How is a guarantee of *equal rights* different from a guarantee of *equality*?

Do you agree with Hamilton that inequality will exist as long as liberty exists? Why or why not?

Consent of the People

"The fabric of American empire ought to rest on the solid basis of THE CONSENT OF THE PEOPLE. The streams of national power ought to flow immediately from that pure, original fountain of all legitimate authority."

Thoughts & Reflections

★ ★ ★ ★

The United States is a *republic*. Under this form of government, representatives elected by the people are accountable to act in the interest of the people who have elected them. The power to govern exists only through the consent of the people. Alexander Hamilton believed that this was the best form of government for a free nation.

Because the United States is a republic, the American people do not directly create the laws that govern our nation. Rather, we elect representatives and give them the consent to act on our behalf. Therefore, in order for the American people to retain their legitimate authority over government—as envisioned by our founders—it is important for citizens to be politically active, speak to their representatives, and exercise their right to vote.

What is a *republic*? What powers does government have in a republic? What powers do citizens have in a republic?

What did Hamilton mean when he stated that national power should flow from the "fountain of all legitimate authority"?

Limited Government

"The injury which may possibly be done by defeating a few good laws, will be amply compensated by the advantage of preventing a number of bad ones."

Thoughts & Reflections

★ ★ ★ ★

Our founding fathers understood, that even in a free society, laws were needed. But it was the objective of Alexander Hamilton and the other framers of our Constitution that the role of government be limited. Our founders understood that while some laws were needed to protect the rights of the American people, laws could also infringe upon these same rights if not carefully conceived. With this in mind, the United States Constitution defines the specific powers and limits to these powers for our federal government.

Under the Constitution, the system of checks and balances that was put in place was intended, in part, to keep government from acting in haste to pass laws without careful deliberation. Alexander Hamilton and others believed that a few bad laws were a greater threat to the American people than the failure of government to pass a few good laws.

———————⌒⌒———————

Do you agree with Hamilton that a few bad laws are a greater threat than the defeat of a few good laws? Why or Why not?

When are laws needed to protect our rights? When do laws infringe upon our rights? Give examples.

Rights of Mankind

"The Sacred Rights of mankind are not to be rummaged for among old parchments or musty records. They are written, as with a sunbeam, in the whole volume of human nature, by the Hand of the Divinity itself; and can never be erased or obscured by mortal power."

Thoughts & Reflections

★ ★ ★ ★

Our founding fathers spoke often about the rights of mankind, which they saw as "unalienable rights." These are rights that cannot be taken away by government. Likewise, these rights are not bestowed upon the people by government.

Alexander Hamilton believed that the rights of mankind are sacred rights that come from a divine source. As stated in the Declaration of Independence, our founders believed that we are endowed by our Creator with certain *unalienable rights*—life, liberty, and the pursuit of happiness.

Our founding fathers were determined to establish a nation that would protect the sacred rights of mankind so that no "mortal power" would erase or obscure these rights.

What are *unalienable rights*? Why can't these rights be "erased or obscured by mortal power"?

What did Hamilton mean that the rights of mankind were written "by the Hand of Divinity itself"?

Samuel Adams

(September 27, 1722 – October 2, 1803)

"*Without the character of Samuel Adams, the true history of the American Revolution can never be written.*"

- John Adams

Samuel Adams is reputed to have once said, *"It does not require a majority to prevail, but rather an irate, tireless minority keen to set brush fires in people's minds."*

Whether or not these are Adams' words, he certainly proved them to be true. In the years leading up to the American Revolution, Samuel Adams was a driving force behind a growing movement that sought independence from Great Britain. As a member of the Massachusetts House of Representatives, Adams spoke out often against British rule over the colonies. And as a member of the Massachusetts Committee of Correspondence, he wrote letters to representatives from the other colonies in an effort to coordinate organized resistance against the British.

Samuel Adams was also believed by some to have played a role in organizing the Boston Tea Party (1773), and he was a prominent figure in the Second Continental Congress (1775–1776). During the historic meetings that convened in Philadelphia, Adams served on four committees (no other delegate served on more than two) and was one of the signers of our Declaration of Independence.

Though he is often overlooked for his role in the founding of our nation, Samuel Adams has come to be regarded by many historians as the "father of the American Revolution."

Liberty

"The natural Liberty of Man is to be free from any superior Power on Earth, and not to be under the Will or Legislative Authority of Man, but only to have the Law of Nature for his Rule."

Thoughts & Reflections

★ ★ ★ ★

Samuel Adams spoke about the "natural liberty of man." By *natural liberty* he meant the liberty granted to us by God. It was the belief of Samuel Adams, as well as the other founders, that no authority on Earth had the power to rule over man. Adams believed that *natural law* should be at the foundation of all laws that govern the affairs of man.

Like many of our other founding fathers, Samuel Adams spoke often about natural law. He believed that all people are governed by certain laws of nature that are based on virtue and moral values. These laws are not created by any person or government. As Adams saw it, these laws are God's laws. Samuel Adams believed that liberty can only exist where the rule of natural law is respected.

What does the term *natural liberty* mean? Where does natural liberty come from?

What is *natural law*? How has a respect for natural law helped to shape the laws of our nation and to protect our liberty?

Citizenship

"*Let each Citizen remember, at the Moment he is offering his Vote, that he is not making a Present or a Compliment to please an Individual, or at least that he ought not so to do; but that he is executing one of the most solemn Trusts in human Society, for which he is accountable to GOD and his Country.*"

Thoughts & Reflections

★ ★ ★ ★

As citizens of a free nation, we have many individual rights. But we also have important responsibilities. While it is our right to vote for our elected leaders, it is also our duty to execute this responsibility with great care. In doing so, we demonstrate our *citizenship*.

Samuel Adams spoke of our responsibility to vote as "one of the most solemn trusts." He saw voting as an important and sacred responsibility. He reminds us that the decisions we make each time we cast a vote require thoughtful and careful consideration. As Adams so plainly stated, when we vote, we are accountable to God and country.

What is the difference between a *right* and a *responsibility*? Why is the act of voting such an important responsibility of each American citizen?

What is *citizenship*? In addition to voting, what are some other responsibilities that demonstrate citizenship?

Property

"*The Utopian schemes of leveling, and a community of goods, are as visionary and impracticable, as those which vest all property in the Crown, are arbitrary, despotic, and in our government unconstitutional. Now, what property can the colonists be conceived to have, if their money may be granted away by others, without their consent?*"

Thoughts & Reflections

★ ★ ★ ★

Under British rule, the American colonists saw much of the fruits of their own labor go to the King of England. Our founding fathers fought for their independence, in large part, so that they could acquire and keep their own property.

Our founding fathers were committed to creating a government that would protect the right of the individual to acquire property and wealth, but they also realized that it was not the proper role of government to divide property and wealth equally among its citizens. Samuel Adams believed that a government that took what belonged to some of its citizens in order to give to others was no better than a king who took from the people for his own benefit.

Do you agree with Samuel Adams that it is not the proper role of government to divide equally, or *level*, the wealth of its citizens by *granting away* their property? Why or Why not?

Virtue

"A general Dissolution of Principles and Manners will more surely overthrow the Liberties of America than the whole Force of the Common Enemy. While the People are virtuous they cannot be subdued; but when once they lose their Virtue they will be ready to surrender their Liberties to the first external or internal Invader."

Thoughts & Reflections

★ ★ ★ ★

Our founding fathers were courageous men who realized that the American colonies did not possess a military force as powerful as the one they faced in fighting for their independence from Great Britain. Nevertheless, they believed there was an honor and strength within the American colonists that would lead them to victory against any enemy of liberty.

Through difficult times, during the early days of the American Revolution, Samuel Adams reminded the American people of the strength that comes from being a virtuous people. Virtue is a quality that unites people in defense of a just cause, such as the cause of liberty. Virtue is a strength that Adams believed could not be subdued. On the other hand, Adams also believed that people without virtue were more of a threat to their own liberty than a common enemy.

───────────⟨∞⟩───────────

How is *virtue* a strength that cannot be subdued?

Why do you think Samuel Adams said that people who lose their virtue "will be ready to surrender their liberties"? Do you agree with this statement?

Freedom

"The right to freedom being the gift of God Almighty, it is not in the power of man to alienate this gift and voluntarily become a slave."

Thoughts & Reflections

★ ★ ★ ★

Though many of our founding fathers were religious men, few possessed the spiritual strength and faith of Samuel Adams. It was the belief that freedom is a gift from God that so greatly inspired Samuel Adams to fight for the independence of our nation.

Samuel Adams believed that the pursuit of freedom is more than an obligation to ourselves—it is an obligation to God.

―――――――――⊃✑⊂―――――――――

Do you agree with Samuel Adams that freedom is a gift from God?

What did Samuel Adams mean when he stated "it is not in the power of man to alienate this gift and voluntarily become a slave"?

Defending Our Constitution

"The liberties of our Country, the freedom of our civil constitution, are worth defending at all hazards; And it is our duty to defend them against all attacks. We have received them as a fair Inheritance from our worthy Ancestors: they purchased them for us with toil and danger and expense of treasure and blood, and transmitted them to us with care and diligence. It will bring an everlasting mark of infamy on the present generation, enlightened as it is, if we should suffer them to be wrested from us by violence without a struggle, or to be cheated out of them by the artifices of false and designing men."

Thoughts & Reflections

★ ★ ★ ★

Many generations of Americans fought and struggled to make our nation a place of liberty and freedom. When our founding fathers succeeded in winning their independence from Great Britain, they sought to secure liberty and freedom for generations to come by establishing a nation and a Constitution worthy of defending.

Samuel Adams believed that he and the other Americans of his generation had a duty to their ancestors to defend liberty and freedom at all costs. If we are to follow his example, it is the duty of every generation of Americans to defend our country and our Constitution—not just as a means to preserve liberty and freedom for the next generation—but to also pay tribute to the efforts of every generation of Americans that has led the way before us.

What are some things that every American can do to defend our Constitution?

Why is defending our Constitution necessary to protecting our liberty and freedom?

Money and Politics

"*I hope our country will never see the time, when either riches or the want of them will be the leading considerations in the choice of public officers.*"

Thoughts & Reflections

★ ★ ★ ★

Samuel Adams had a noble vision for the government of the United States. He saw the act of governing as a service to our nation, not to be limited to a select few, but to any qualified individuals who possess leadership skills.

Under British rule, the founding fathers had grown accustomed to seeing only individuals with great wealth or ties to royalty in positions of power. Samuel Adams hoped that the United States would follow a different path. Adams, as well as many other founding fathers, did not possess great wealth. He realized that money alone did not make great leaders. In fact, Adams understood that money could possibly corrupt government. He believed it was most important to elect people of great character and skill to public office, whether wealthy or not.

—————————⊃✑⊂—————————

How can money corrupt government? Can you think of examples of when this has happened?

What considerations should be most important when electing people to public office?

Peace

"*If you carefully fulfill the various Duties of Life, from a Principle of Obedience to your heavenly Father, you shall enjoy that Peace which the World cannot give nor take away.*"

Thoughts & Reflections

★ ★ ★ ★

The word *peace* is often used to mean "free from conflict or disagreement." But Samuel Adams understood that true peace has more to do with internal feelings than external forces. As a religious man, Adams believed that true peace could only be found by serving God.

During difficult times throughout the American Revolution, Samuel Adams found comfort in knowing that the cause of the American people was a just cause. He believed it was his obligation to defend freedom and liberty. Though it was a time of much conflict and disagreement, Adams knew that it was still possible to find true peace by fulfilling "the various Duties of Life." To Samuel Adams, defending the unalienable, God-given rights of the American people was one of these duties.

What do you think Samuel Adams meant by "Duties of Life"? What are your "Duties of Life"?

What things bring you peace even during difficult times?

Thomas Paine

(February 9, 1737 – June 8, 1809)

"The citizens of the United States cannot look back upon the time of their own revolution without recollecting among the names of their most distinguished patriots, that of Thomas Paine."

\- James Monroe

Thomas Paine did not sign the Declaration of Independence; he did not help to draft our Constitution; he was not an accomplished politician; and he never became a great war hero. It was as a voice of the common man that Thomas Paine left his mark on history.

Thomas Paine first arrived in America in 1774 and quickly made his presence known. As a gifted writer, he stirred the hearts and minds of the American people during difficult times as they struggled for their independence. In 1776, Paine published a pamphlet titled *Common Sense*. The pamphlet was one of the first public calls for a formal declaration of independence from Great Britain. It had a profound impact on public opinion and rallied many colonists to the cause.

During the American Revolution, Paine again inspired the American people with a series of pamphlets titled *The Crisis* (1776–1783). In his writings, Paine urged American patriots to continue their virtuous struggle despite the challenges.

When the American Revolution ended, Paine traveled to Europe and continued to be a voice for the common man in places where the struggle for liberty continued. He then returned to the United States in 1802 and lived his remaining years in relative obscurity. Today, he is well remembered for the role he played in the founding of our nation.

Courage

"*I love the man that can smile in trouble, that can gather strength from distress, and grow brave by reflection. 'Tis the business of little minds to shrink; but he whose heart is firm, and whose conscience approves his conduct, will pursue his principles unto death.*"

Thoughts & Reflections

★ ★ ★ ★

In the years leading up to the American Revolution, Thomas Paine was one of the first founding fathers to boldly call for the American colonists to revolt against the British. He published many papers that angered the British and inspired the colonists. Like our other founding fathers, Thomas Paine was a man of action. He not only played a role in inspiring the American people to fight for their independence, but several years later went to France in support of the French Revolution.

Thomas Paine greatly admired those who were willing to stand up and fight for principles. He believed that such people drew their courage from the beliefs that they held within their hearts.

Are you a person of action? What are some things that you have done that required courage?

How does a person "gather strength from distress" and "grow brave by reflection"?

Self-Sacrifice

"If there must be trouble, let it be in my day, that my child may have peace."

Thoughts & Reflections

★ ★ ★ ★

Like the other founding fathers, Thomas Paine was concerned about more than his own self-interests. Thomas Paine was willing to endure difficult times so that future generations would not have to.

Our founding fathers did not just fight for their own independence and their own liberty. They fought for the independence and liberty of all Americans for generations to come. They were willing to sacrifice peace in their time so that their children, and their children's children, could live in peace.

———————⊃◦∽◦⊂———————

Can you think of times when you have made sacrifices for others?

What would you be willing to do to protect the freedom and liberty of your children (or others)?

Who are some people you know that put the needs and interests of others first? What actions have they taken for you (or others)?

Freedom

"*Those who expect to reap the blessings of freedom, must, like men, undergo the fatigues of supporting it.*"

Thoughts & Reflections

★ ★ ★ ★

Throughout history, people have had to struggle and fight for their freedom. Thomas Paine understood that freedom is rarely free—it often comes at a great price. During the American Revolution, thousands of people died fighting for their freedom. Many years later, hundreds of thousands of people died in the struggle to end slavery during the Civil War. Even today, the struggle for freedom still goes on in many places throughout the world.

Our founding fathers knew the value of freedom and the cost at which it comes. Even during times of peace we must not forget how precious freedom is. As Thomas Paine reminds us, we must stand ready to "undergo the fatigues of supporting it."

What does *freedom* mean to you?

Have you ever had to defend or "undergo the fatigues of supporting" freedom? Can you think of someone who has?

Government

"*Society in every state is a blessing, but Government even in its best state is but a necessary evil; in its worst state an intolerable one.*"

Thoughts & Reflections

★ ★ ★ ★

In order to adequately protect the interests and rights of the people in a free society, our founding fathers realized that some form of government was needed. But our founders also knew that it was impossible to establish a government without asking the people to surrender authority and power to others. For this reason, Thomas Paine saw government as a "necessary evil."

Our founding fathers were always mindful of the need to limit the amount of power entrusted to those who would govern. With this in mind, the Constitution was written to establish a clearly defined and limited role for a federal government.

What did Thomas Paine mean when he stated that a government in its best state is a "necessary evil" and in its worst state an "intolerable one"? Do you agree with this statement?

Principles

"*An army of principles will penetrate where an army of soldiers cannot ... It will march on the horizon of the world, and it will conquer.*"

Thoughts & Reflections

★ ★ ★ ★

Principles are beliefs that guide us. They give us the strength and clarity of mind to know what course of action to take in all situations.

One of the principles in which our founding fathers believed is that *all men are endowed by their Creator with certain unalienable rights*. They believed that these unalienable rights include *life, liberty, and the pursuit of happiness*. It was these beliefs that inspired our founding fathers to fight for their independence.

Thomas Paine believed in the cause of the American Revolution because he knew that the American people would stand firmly on principles of liberty and freedom. These guiding principles were enough, Paine believed, to lead the American people to victory.

What principles guide your actions?

What principles, or beliefs, do you think you share with our founding fathers?

Oppression

"He that would make his own liberty secure, must guard even his enemy from oppression; for if he violates this duty, he establishes a precedent that will reach to himself."

Thoughts & Reflections

★ ★ ★ ★

Following the American Revolution, Thomas Paine realized that there were still many places in the world where people lived in oppression. Paine believed that those fortunate enough to enjoy the comforts of liberty had an obligation to help those who were oppressed.

Thomas Paine continued to fight for the cause of liberty long after the American Revolution ended. He argued that if a nation of free people failed to help others who are oppressed, it would put their own liberty at risk. By defending liberty at all times and in all places, Thomas Paine believed, the American people would become more secure against threats to their own liberty.

What does it mean to live in oppression?

Why is it important for those who enjoy liberty to help those who are oppressed?

In Times of Crisis

"These are the times that try men's souls. The summer soldier and the sunshine patriot will, in this crisis, shrink from the service of their country; but he that stands by it now, deserves the love and thanks of man and woman. Tyranny, like hell, is not easily conquered; yet we have this consolation with us, that the harder the conflict, the more glorious the triumph. What we obtain too cheap, we esteem too lightly: 'Tis dearness only that gives every thing its value. Heaven knows how to put a proper price upon its goods; and it would be strange indeed if so celestial an article as FREEDOM should not be highly rated."

Thoughts & Reflections

★ ★ ★ ★

At the start of the American Revolution, things did not go well for the colonists, and many began to doubt the war could be won. It was against this backdrop that Thomas Paine published a series of papers he called *The Crisis*. His impassioned plea to continue the struggle for independence began with the memorable words "These are the times that try men's souls." He went on to speak about the "summer soldier" and the "sunshine patriot"—those who stand strong and proud during goods times but are silent and unwilling to act during difficult times.

During the harsh, cold winter of 1776, as George Washington prepared to lead his troops across the Delaware River and again into battle, he sought to lift their spirits and ordered that Thomas Paine's words be read to every regiment of soldiers. Inspired by these words, Washington and his troops went on to win a series of key battles.

⊃◈⊂

What did Paine mean when he said "what we obtain too cheap, we esteem too lightly"?

During difficult times, what are you willing to do for your country?

Final Thoughts

Much of our life experience has conditioned us to become passive learners. All too often we acquire only the knowledge that is presented to us. But to be good stewards of the blessings of liberty, much more is required. We must actively seek knowledge that will lead us to truth and a greater understanding of our heritage as Americans. If the principles and values of our founding fathers are to endure, it is the responsibility of each one of us to pass on their wisdom and passion to the next generation. We must remember their words and not allow them to be erased by time.

Do not look to others to secure your blessing of liberty, but look to yourself. You can make a difference. Educating yourself and arming yourself with knowledge is just the first step. The next step is what you do with the knowledge you have acquired.

Benjamin Franklin once said:

"All mankind is divided into three classes: those that are immovable, those that are movable, and those that move."

Which type of person will you choose to be?

Sources and References

Artworks

p. 4   *Declaration of Independence:*
        Original painting by John Trumbull
        (Courtesy of Wikimedia Commons).

p. 16   *Scene at the Signing of the Constitution of the
        United States:*
        Original painting by Howard Chandler Christy
        (Courtesy of Wikimedia Commons).

p. 28   *Drafting of the Declaration of Independence:*
        Original painting by Alonzo Chappel
        (Courtesy of Wikimedia Commons).

p. 32   *George Washington:*
        Original painting by Peter Frederick Rothermel;
        engraving by Alexander Hay Ritchie
        (Courtesy of the Library of Congress).

p. 56   *John Adams:*
        Original painting by Gilbert Stuart;
        lithograph by Pendleton's Lithography
        (Courtesy of the Library of Congress).

p. 80   *Thomas Jefferson:*
        Original painting by Gilbert Stuart
        (Courtesy of the Library of Congress).

p. 102 *Benjamin Franklin:*
        Original painting by Joseph-Siffred Duplessis;
        engraving by H.B. Hall
        (Courtesy of the Library of Congress).

p. 118 *James Madison:*
        Original painting by Gilbert Stuart;
        lithograph by Pendleton's Lithography
        (Courtesy of the Library of Congress).

Principal Quotes (quotes in bold type)

George Washington

195

James Madison

Alexander Hamilton

Samuel Adams

Thomas Paine

<u>Additional Quotes</u> (quotes that appear in this book in addition to the principal quotes in bold type)

The quote on the page following the acknowledgment page (no page number) is by Dr. Henry Stuber as part of a biographical sketch of Benjamin Franklin that was appended to a 1793 Franklin autobiography titled *Works of the Late Doctor Benjamin Franklin* (p.97).

p. 2   Niccolò Machiavelli, *The Discources*; 1517.

p. 6   The quote "*We must all hang together, or assuredly we shall all hang separately*" has been attributed to Benjamin Franklin at the signing of the Declaration of Independence; 1776.

p. 32   Letter to Dr. Walter Jones from Thomas Jefferson (about George Washington); January 2, 1814.

p. 56   Letter to Jacques Barbeu-Dubourg from Benjamin Rush (about John Adams); September 16, 1776.

p. 80   Letter to Henry Pierce and others from Abraham Lincoln; April 6, 1859.

p. 81   Quote: "*The God who gave us life, gave us liberty at the same time: the hand of force may destroy, but cannot disjoin them.*" From *A Summary View of the Rights of British America* by Thomas Jefferson; 1774.

p. 102   English translation of an inscription on a Benjamin Franklin sculpture by Anne Robert Jacques Turgot; 1778.

p. 105   Quote: *"henceforth prayers imploring the assistance of Heaven, and its blessings on our deliberations, be held in this Assembly every morning."* From a speech by Benjamin Franklin to the delegates at the Constitutional Convention on June 28, 1787.

p. 118   *An Eulogy on the Life and Character of James Madison* (p. 4) by John Quincy Adams; September 27, 1836.

p. 144   Henry Cabot Lodge to James M. Beck; July 17, 1923.

p. 156   Letter to William Tudor from John Adams; June 5, 1817.

p. 157   The quote *"It does not require a majority to prevail, but rather an irate, tireless minority keen to set brush fires in people's minds"* has been attributed to Samuel Adams. Original source unknown; secondary source: Bob Gingrich, *Founding Fathers vs. History Revisionists* (p.104); AuthorHouse, 2008.

p. 174   Letter to the Committee of General Surety from James Monroe; November 1, 1794.

p. 191   The quote *"All mankind is divided into three classes: those that are immovable, those that are movable, and those that move"* is an Arabian proverb quoted by Benjamin Franklin. Original source unknown; secondary source: Montgomery Van Wart, *Dynamics of Leadership in Public Service* (p. 74); M.E, Sharp Inc., 2005.

Research

Historical Documents

The Declaration of Independence (1776)
The United States Constitution (1787)
The Bill of Rights (1789)
The Federalist Papers (1787–1788)

Books

Adams, John. *The Works of John Adams*, 10 vols. Edited by Charles Francis Adams. Boston: Little Brown and Co., 1856.

Adams, John Quincy. *An Eulogy on the Life and Character of James Madison*. Boston: John H. Eastburn, 1836.

Adams, Samuel. *The Writings of Samuel Adams*, 4 vols. Edited by Harry Alonzo Cushing. New York and London: G.P. Putnam's Sons, 1904–1908.

Ellis, Joseph J. *Founding Brothers: The Revolutionary Generation*. New York: Vintage Books, 2000.

Flexner, James Thomas. *Washington: The Indispensable Man*. New York: Back Bay Books, 1974.

Franklin, Benjamin. *Memoirs of Benjamin Franklin*, 2 vols. New York: Derby & Jackson, 1859.

Franklin, Benjamin. *Works of the Late Doctor Benjamin Franklin*. Dublin: Wogan, Byrne, Moore, & Jones, 1793.

Hamilton, Alexander. *The Works of Alexander Hamilton*, 12 vols. Edited by Henry Cabot Lodge. New York: G.P. Putnam's Sons, 1904.

Jefferson, Thomas. *The Works of Thomas Jefferson*, 12 vols. Edited by Paul Leicester Ford. New York and London: G.P. Putnam's Sons, 1904–1905.

Holler, Michael. *The Constitution Made Easy.* Woodland Park, Colorado: The Friends of Freedom, 2008.

Madison, James. *The Writings of James Madison*, 9 vols. Edited by Gaillard Hunt. New York: G.P. Putnam's Sons, 1900.

Paine, Thomas. *The Writings of Thomas Paine*, 4 vols. Edited by Moncure Daniel Conway. New York: G.P. Putnam's Sons, 1894.

Peacock, Anthony A. *How to Read the Federalist Papers.* Washington, D.C.: The Heritage Foundation, 2010.

Skousen, W. Cleon. *The 5000 Year Leap: A Miracle That Changed the World.* National Center for Constitutional Studies, 2006.

Stewart, David O. *The Summer of 1787: The Men Who Invented the Constitution.* New York: Simon and Schuster, 2007.

Stoll, Ira. *Samuel Adams: A Life.* New York: Free Press, 2008.

Washington, George. *George Washington: A Collection.* Edited by William B. Allen. Indianapolis: Liberty Fund, 1988.

Websites

ConstitutionFacts.com
http://www.constitutionfacts.com/

Constitution Society
http://www.constitution.org/

Encyclopedia Britannica
http://www.britannica.com/

FoundingFathers.info
http://www.foundingfathers.info/

Founding Father Quotes
http://www.foundingfatherquotes.com/

Gilder Lehrman Institute of American History
http://www.gilderlehrman.org/

Google Books
http://books.google.com/

Liberty Fund Online Library of Liberty
http://oll.libertyfund.org/

Library of Congress
http://www.loc.gov/

Mark's Quotes: Founding Fathers Quotes
http://www.marksquotes.com/Founding-Fathers/

National Archives
http://www.archives.gov/

We Still Hold These Truths: Quotes Database
http://www.westillholdthesetruths.org/quotes

Notes

Dates of birth indicated for George Washington (p. 32), John Adams (p. 56), Thomas Jefferson (p. 80), Benjamin Franklin (p. 102), James Madison (p. 118), Samuel Adams (p. 156), and Thomas Paine (p. 174) are New Style dates. In 1752, the British colonies changed from the Julian (old style) calendar to the Gregorian (new style) calendar. Old Style dates of birth are as follows: George Washington, February 11, 1732; John Adams, October 19, 1735; Thomas Jefferson, April 2, 1743; Benjamin Franklin, January 6, 1706; James Madison, March 5, 1751; Samuel Adams, September 16, 1722; Thomas Paine, January 29, 1737.

Capitalization of words from original source documents, such as excerpts from the Declaration of Independence and the United States Constitution, has been retained although this may deviate from modern conventions.

The quotation that appears on page 140 is from Federalist Paper Number 62. Most historians credit James Madison with writing this document. However, some historians have attributed the document to Alexander Hamilton.

The quotations contained in this book have been verified using multiple sources (see pages 200–202). However, it should be noted that similar variants of some quotes have been cited in other works.

The American Dream Lives!